A Let's-Read-and-Find-Out-Book™

Revised Edition

MY FIVE SENSES
by
ALIKI

A TRUMPET CLUB SPECIAL EDITION

Let's-Read-and-Find-Out Science Book is a registered
trademark of HarperCollins Publishers

Published by The Trumpet Club
666 Fifth Avenue, New York, New York 10103

Copyright © 1962, 1989 by Aliki Brandenberg

ISBN: 0-440-84354-5

This edition published by arrangement with
HarperCollins Publishers
Printed in the United States of America
September 1991

UPC   10 9 8 7 6 5 4 3 2 1

The *Let's-Read-and-Find-Out Science Book* series was originated by Dr. Franklyn M. Branley, Astronomer
Emeritus and former Chairman of the American Museum-Hayden Planetarium, and was formerly co-edited by
him and Dr. Roma Gans, Professor Emeritus of Childhood Education, Teachers College, Columbia University.

MY FIVE SENSES

for my sister, Helen Lambros

I can see! I see with my eyes.

I can hear! I hear with my ears.

I can smell! I smell with my nose.

I can taste! I taste with my tongue.

I can touch! I touch with my fingers.

13

I do all this with my senses.
I have five senses.

When I see the sun or a frog

or my baby sister,

I use my sense of sight. I am seeing.

When I hear a drum or a fire engine
or a bird,
I use my sense of hearing.
I am hearing.

When I smell soap or a pine tree
or cookies just out of the oven,
I use my sense of smell.
I am smelling.

When I drink my milk
and eat my food,
I use my sense of taste.
I am tasting.

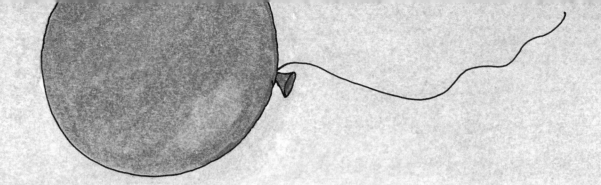

When I touch a kitten or a balloon or water,

I use my sense of touch.

I am touching.

19

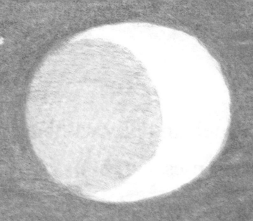

Sometimes I use all my senses at once.

Sometimes I use only one.

I often play a game with myself.

I guess how many senses I am using at that time.

When I look at the moon and the stars,

I use one sense.

I am seeing.

When I laugh and play with my puppy,

I use four senses.

I see, hear, smell, and touch.

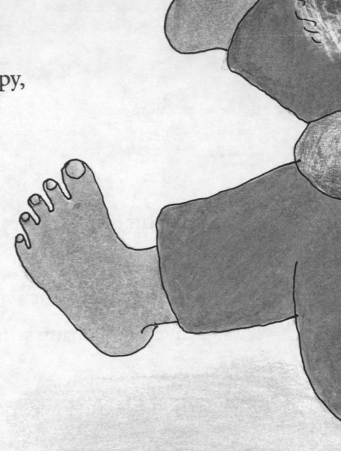

When I bounce a ball, I use three senses.

I see, hear, touch.

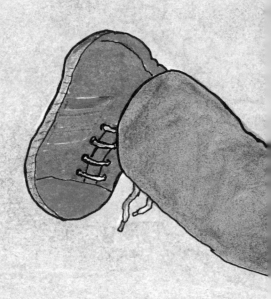

Sometimes I use more of one sense
and less of another.
But each sense is very important to me,
because it makes me aware.

To be aware is to see all there is to see...

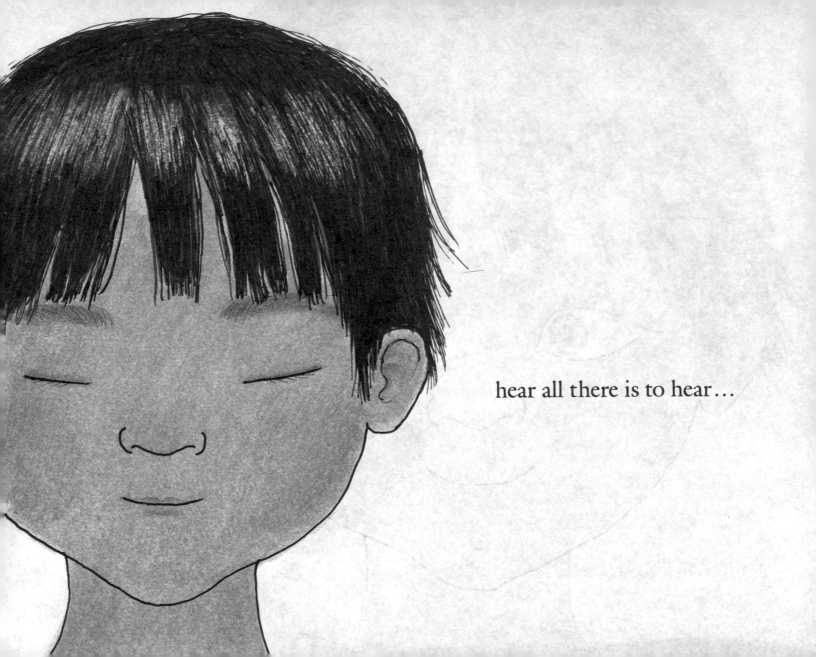

hear all there is to hear...

smell all there is to smell…

taste all there is to taste...

30

touch all there is to touch.

Wherever I go, whatever I do,
every minute of the day,
my senses are working.

They make me aware.